NAME:

HIKING LOGBOOK

"Travel makes one modest.
You see what a tiny place
you occupy in the World."
–Gustave Flaubert

HIKING LOGBOOK

DATE: ☀ ⛅ ☁ 🌧 ⛈ ❄ 🌫 ☐Hot ☐Cold ☐Mild

Start Time:_____ End Time:_____

Total Duration:_____ Total Distance:_____

Elevation Gain/Loss:_____

Trail Type (circle one):   Out & Back   Loop   One Way / Shuttle

THE HIKE   ☆ ☆ ☆ ☆ ☆

City/State:_____

Trail(s):_____

_____

Start Latitude/Longitude:_____

Terrain:_____

Cell Phone Reception/Carrier:_____

☐First Visit   ☐Return Visit   Personal Rating: Easy / Intermediate / Difficult

Companion(s):_____

Facilities / Water Availability?:_____

Trail & Weather Conditions:_____

Observances (wildlife, nature, views, etc):_____

Gear, Food & Beverages:_____

Notes for next time (shuttles, entrance fees, parking, routes, pets, etc):_____

_____

NOTES / JOURNALING

HIKING LOGBOOK

DATE: ☀ ⛅ ☁ 🌧 ⛈ ❄ 🌬 ☐Hot ☐Cold ☐Mild

Start Time:_____ End Time:_____

Total Duration:_____ Total Distance:_____

Elevation Gain/Loss:_____

Trail Type (circle one):   Out & Back   Loop   One Way / Shuttle

THE HIKE ☆☆☆☆☆

City/State:_____

Trail(s):_____

_____

Start Latitude/Longitude:_____

Terrain:_____

Cell Phone Reception/Carrier:_____

☐First Visit ☐Return Visit   Personal Rating: Easy / Intermediate / Difficult

Companion(s):_____

_____

Facilities / Water Availability?:_____

_____

Trail & Weather Conditions:_____

_____

Observances (wildlife, nature, views, etc):_____

_____

Gear, Food & Beverages:_____

_____

Notes for next time (shuttles, entrance fees, parking, routes, pets, etc):_____

_____

_____

NOTES / JOURNALING

HIKING LOGBOOK

DATE: ☀ ⛅ ☁ 🌧 ⛈ ❄ 🌫 ☐Hot ☐Cold ☐Mild

Start Time:_____ End Time:_____

Total Duration:_____ Total Distance:_____

Elevation Gain/Loss:_____

Trail Type (circle one):   Out & Back   Loop   One Way / Shuttle

THE HIKE   ☆☆☆☆☆

City/State:_____

Trail(s):_____
_____

Start Latitude/Longitude:_____

Terrain:_____

Cell Phone Reception/Carrier:_____

☐First Visit ☐Return Visit   Personal Rating: Easy / Intermediate / Difficult

Companion(s):_____

Facilities / Water Availability?:_____

Trail & Weather Conditions:_____

Observances (wildlife, nature, views, etc):_____

Gear, Food & Beverages:_____

Notes for next time (shuttles, entrance fees, parking, routes, pets, etc):_____

NOTES / JOURNALING

HIKING LOGBOOK

DATE: ☀ ⛅ ☁ 🌧 ⛈ ❄ 🌫 ☐Hot ☐Cold ☐Mild

Start Time:_____ End Time:_____

Total Duration:_____ Total Distance:_____

Elevation Gain/Loss:_____

Trail Type (circle one):   Out & Back   Loop   One Way / Shuttle

THE HIKE ☆ ☆ ☆ ☆ ☆

City/State:_____

Trail(s):_____
_____

Start Latitude/Longitude:_____

Terrain:_____

Cell Phone Reception/Carrier:_____

☐First Visit ☐Return Visit   Personal Rating: Easy / Intermediate / Difficult

Companion(s):_____
_____

Facilities / Water Availability?:_____
_____

Trail & Weather Conditions:_____
_____

Observances (wildlife, nature, views, etc):_____
_____

Gear, Food & Beverages:_____
_____

Notes for next time (shuttles, entrance fees, parking, routes, pets, etc):_____
_____
_____

NOTES / JOURNALING

HIKING LOGBOOK

DATE: ☼ ⛅ ☁ 🌧 ⛈ ❄ 🌬 ☐Hot ☐Cold ☐Mild

Start Time:_____ End Time:_____

Total Duration:_____ Total Distance:_____

Elevation Gain/Loss:_____

Trail Type (circle one):   Out & Back   Loop   One Way / Shuttle

THE HIKE ☆☆☆☆☆

City/State:_____

Trail(s):_____

Start Latitude/Longitude:_____

Terrain:_____

Cell Phone Reception/Carrier:_____

☐First Visit   ☐Return Visit   Personal Rating: Easy / Intermediate / Difficult

Companion(s):_____

Facilities / Water Availability?:_____

Trail & Weather Conditions:_____

Observances (wildlife, nature, views, etc):_____

Gear, Food & Beverages:_____

Notes for next time (shuttles, entrance fees, parking, routes, pets, etc):_____

NOTES / JOURNALING

HIKING LOGBOOK

DATE: ☼ ⛅ ☁ 🌧 ⛈ ❄ 🌬 ☐ Hot ☐ Cold ☐ Mild

Start Time:_____ End Time:_____

Total Duration:_____ Total Distance:_____

Elevation Gain/Loss:_____

Trail Type (circle one):   Out & Back   Loop   One Way / Shuttle

THE HIKE ☆☆☆☆☆

City/State:_____

Trail(s):_____
_____

Start Latitude/Longitude:_____

Terrain:_____

Cell Phone Reception/Carrier:_____

☐First Visit   ☐Return Visit   Personal Rating: Easy / Intermediate / Difficult

Companion(s):_____

Facilities / Water Availability?:_____

Trail & Weather Conditions:_____
_____

Observances (wildlife, nature, views, etc):_____
_____

Gear, Food & Beverages:_____
_____

Notes for next time (shuttles, entrance fees, parking, routes, pets, etc):_____
_____
_____

NOTES / JOURNALING

HIKING LOGBOOK

DATE: ☼ ⛅ ☁ ☂ ⛆ ❄ 🌬 ☐Hot ☐Cold ☐Mild

Start Time:_____ End Time:_____

Total Duration:_____ Total Distance:_____

Elevation Gain/Loss:_____

Trail Type (circle one):   Out & Back   Loop   One Way / Shuttle

THE HIKE   ☆ ☆ ☆ ☆ ☆

City/State:_____

Trail(s):_____

_____

Start Latitude/Longitude:_____

Terrain:_____

Cell Phone Reception/Carrier:_____

☐First Visit   ☐Return Visit   Personal Rating: Easy / Intermediate / Difficult

Companion(s):_____

Facilities / Water Availability?:_____

Trail & Weather Conditions:_____

Observances (wildlife, nature, views, etc):_____

Gear, Food & Beverages:_____

Notes for next time (shuttles, entrance fees, parking, routes, pets, etc):_____

_____

NOTES / JOURNALING

HIKING LOGBOOK

DATE: ☼ ⛅ ☁ ☂ ⛈ ❄ 🌬 ☐Hot ☐Cold ☐Mild

Start Time:_____ End Time:_____

Total Duration:_____ Total Distance:_____

Elevation Gain/Loss:_____

Trail Type (circle one):   Out & Back   Loop   One Way / Shuttle

THE HIKE   ☆ ☆ ☆ ☆ ☆

City/State:_____

Trail(s):_____

Start Latitude/Longitude:_____

Terrain:_____

Cell Phone Reception/Carrier:_____

☐First Visit   ☐Return Visit   Personal Rating: Easy / Intermediate / Difficult

Companion(s):_____

Facilities / Water Availability?:_____

Trail & Weather Conditions:_____

Observances (wildlife, nature, views, etc):_____

Gear, Food & Beverages:_____

Notes for next time (shuttles, entrance fees, parking, routes, pets, etc):_____

NOTES / JOURNALING

HIKING LOGBOOK

DATE: ☀ ⛅ ☁ 🌧 ⛈ ❄ 🌬 ☐Hot ☐Cold ☐Mild

Start Time:_____ **End Time:**_____

Total Duration:_____ **Total Distance:**_____

Elevation Gain/Loss:_____

Trail Type (circle one): Out & Back Loop One Way / Shuttle

THE HIKE   ☆ ☆ ☆ ☆ ☆

City/State:_____

Trail(s):_____

_____

Start Latitude/Longitude:_____

Terrain:_____

Cell Phone Reception/Carrier:_____

☐First Visit ☐Return Visit   **Personal Rating: Easy / Intermediate / Difficult**

Companion(s):_____

Facilities / Water Availability?:_____

Trail & Weather Conditions:_____

Observances (wildlife, nature, views, etc):_____

Gear, Food & Beverages:_____

Notes for next time (shuttles, entrance fees, parking, routes, pets, etc):_____

_____

DATE: ☀ ⛅ ☁ 🌦 🌧 ⛈ ❄ 🌫 ☐Hot ☐Cold ☐Mild

Start Time:_____ End Time:_____

Total Duration:_____ Total Distance:_____

Elevation Gain/Loss:_____

Trail Type (circle one):   Out & Back   Loop   One Way / Shuttle

THE HIKE   ☆ ☆ ☆ ☆ ☆

City/State:_____

Trail(s):_____
_____

Start Latitude/Longitude:_____

Terrain:_____

Cell Phone Reception/Carrier:_____

☐First Visit   ☐Return Visit   Personal Rating: Easy / Intermediate / Difficult

Companion(s):_____

Facilities / Water Availability?:_____

Trail & Weather Conditions:_____

Observances (wildlife, nature, views, etc):_____

Gear, Food & Beverages:_____

Notes for next time (shuttles, entrance fees, parking, routes, pets, etc):_____

NOTES / JOURNALING

HIKING LOGBOOK

DATE: ☼ ⛅ ☁ ☂ ☔ ❄ ☁ □Hot □Cold □Mild

Start Time: _____ End Time: _____

Total Duration: _____ Total Distance: _____

Elevation Gain/Loss: _____

Trail Type (circle one):　Out & Back　Loop　One Way / Shuttle

THE HIKE　　　　　☆ ☆ ☆ ☆ ☆

City/State: _____

Trail(s): _____

_____

Start Latitude/Longitude: _____

Terrain: _____

Cell Phone Reception/Carrier: _____

□First Visit　□Return Visit　Personal Rating: Easy / Intermediate / Difficult

Companion(s): _____

_____

Facilities / Water Availability?: _____

_____

Trail & Weather Conditions: _____

_____

Observances (wildlife, nature, views, etc): _____

_____

Gear, Food & Beverages: _____

_____

Notes for next time (shuttles, entrance fees, parking, routes, pets, etc): _____

_____

_____

NOTES / JOURNALING

DATE: ☀ ⛅ ☁ ☁ 🌧 ❄ 🌫 ☐Hot ☐Cold ☐Mild

Start Time:_____ End Time:_____

Total Duration: _____Total Distance: _____

Elevation Gain/Loss: _____

Trail Type (circle one):   Out & Back   Loop   One Way / Shuttle

THE HIKE   ☆ ☆ ☆ ☆ ☆

City/State:_____

Trail(s):_____

_____

Start Latitude/Longitude: _____

Terrain: _____

Cell Phone Reception/Carrier: _____

☐First Visit   ☐Return Visit   Personal Rating: Easy / Intermediate / Difficult

Companion(s): _____

_____

Facilities / Water Availability?:_____

_____

Trail & Weather Conditions: _____

_____

Observances (wildlife, nature, views, etc):_____

_____

Gear, Food & Beverages: _____

_____

Notes for next time (shuttles, entrance fees, parking, routes, pets, etc):_____

_____

_____

NOTES / JOURNALING

DATE: ☀ ⛅ ☁ 🌧 ⛈ ❄ 🌫 ☐Hot ☐Cold ☐Mild

Start Time:_____ End Time:_____

Total Duration:_____ Total Distance:_____

Elevation Gain/Loss:_____

Trail Type (circle one):   Out & Back   Loop   One Way / Shuttle

THE HIKE   ☆ ☆ ☆ ☆ ☆

City/State:_____

Trail(s):_____

_____

Start Latitude/Longitude:_____

Terrain:_____

Cell Phone Reception/Carrier:_____

☐First Visit   ☐Return Visit   Personal Rating: Easy / Intermediate / Difficult

Companion(s):_____

_____

Facilities / Water Availability?:_____

_____

Trail & Weather Conditions:_____

_____

Observances (wildlife, nature, views, etc):_____

_____

Gear, Food & Beverages:_____

_____

Notes for next time (shuttles, entrance fees, parking, routes, pets, etc):_____

_____

_____

HIKING LOGBOOK

DATE: ☀ ⛅ ☁ 🌧 ⛈ ❄ 🌫 ☐Hot ☐Cold ☐Mild

Start Time:_____ End Time:_____

Total Duration:_____ Total Distance:_____

Elevation Gain/Loss:_____

Trail Type (circle one):   Out & Back   Loop   One Way / Shuttle

THE HIKE ☆ ☆ ☆ ☆ ☆

City/State:_____

Trail(s):_____
_____

Start Latitude/Longitude:_____

Terrain:_____

Cell Phone Reception/Carrier:_____

☐First Visit   ☐Return Visit   Personal Rating: Easy / Intermediate / Difficult

Companion(s):_____
_____

Facilities / Water Availability?:_____
_____

Trail & Weather Conditions:_____
_____

Observances (wildlife, nature, views, etc):_____
_____

Gear, Food & Beverages:_____
_____

Notes for next time (shuttles, entrance fees, parking, routes, pets, etc):_____
_____
_____

HIKING LOGBOOK

DATE: ☼ ⛅ ☁ ☁ 🌧 ⛈ ❄ 🌬 ☐Hot ☐Cold ☐Mild

Start Time:_____ End Time:_____

Total Duration:_____ Total Distance:_____

Elevation Gain/Loss:_____

Trail Type (circle one):   Out & Back   Loop   One Way / Shuttle

THE HIKE   ☆☆☆☆☆

City/State:_____

Trail(s):_____

_____

Start Latitude/Longitude:_____

Terrain:_____

Cell Phone Reception/Carrier:_____

☐First Visit   ☐Return Visit   Personal Rating: Easy / Intermediate / Difficult

Companion(s):_____

_____

Facilities / Water Availability?:_____

_____

Trail & Weather Conditions:_____

_____

Observances (wildlife, nature, views, etc):_____

_____

Gear, Food & Beverages:_____

_____

Notes for next time (shuttles, entrance fees, parking, routes, pets, etc):_____

_____

_____

NOTES / JOURNALING

HIKING LOGBOOK

DATE: ☼ ⛅ ☁ 🌧 ⛈ ❄ 🌬 ☐Hot ☐Cold ☐Mild

Start Time:_____ End Time:_____

Total Duration:_____ Total Distance:_____

Elevation Gain/Loss:_____

Trail Type (circle one):   Out & Back   Loop   One Way / Shuttle

THE HIKE   ☆☆☆☆☆

City/State:_____

Trail(s):_____

_____

Start Latitude/Longitude:_____

Terrain:_____

Cell Phone Reception/Carrier:_____

☐First Visit   ☐Return Visit   Personal Rating: Easy / Intermediate / Difficult

Companion(s):_____

_____

Facilities / Water Availability?:_____

_____

Trail & Weather Conditions:_____

_____

Observances (wildlife, nature, views, etc):_____

_____

Gear, Food & Beverages:_____

_____

Notes for next time (shuttles, entrance fees, parking, routes, pets, etc):_____

_____

NOTES / JOURNALING

HIKING LOGBOOK

DATE: ☼ ⛅ ☁ ☂ ⛈ ❄ 🌬 ☐Hot ☐Cold ☐Mild

Start Time:_____ End Time:_____

Total Duration:_____ Total Distance:_____

Elevation Gain/Loss:_____

Trail Type (circle one):   Out & Back   Loop   One Way / Shuttle

THE HIKE ☆☆☆☆☆

City/State:_____

Trail(s):_____

Start Latitude/Longitude:_____

Terrain:_____

Cell Phone Reception/Carrier:_____

☐First Visit   ☐Return Visit   Personal Rating: Easy / Intermediate / Difficult

Companion(s):_____

Facilities / Water Availability?:_____

Trail & Weather Conditions:_____

Observances (wildlife, nature, views, etc):_____

Gear, Food & Beverages:_____

Notes for next time (shuttles, entrance fees, parking, routes, pets, etc):_____

NOTES / JOURNALING

HIKING LOGBOOK

DATE: ☼ ⛅ ☁ 🌧 ⛈ ❄ 🌫 ☐Hot ☐Cold ☐Mild

Start Time:_____ End Time:_____

Total Duration:_____ Total Distance:_____

Elevation Gain/Loss:_____

Trail Type (circle one):   Out & Back   Loop   One Way / Shuttle

THE HIKE   ☆ ☆ ☆ ☆ ☆

City/State:_____

Trail(s):_____

_____

Start Latitude/Longitude:_____

Terrain:_____

Cell Phone Reception/Carrier:_____

☐First Visit   ☐Return Visit   Personal Rating: Easy / Intermediate / Difficult

Companion(s):_____

_____

Facilities / Water Availability?:_____

_____

Trail & Weather Conditions:_____

_____

Observances (wildlife, nature, views, etc):_____

_____

Gear, Food & Beverages:_____

_____

Notes for next time (shuttles, entrance fees, parking, routes, pets, etc):_____

_____

_____

HIKING LOGBOOK

DATE: ☀ ⛅ ☁ ☁ 🌧 ❄ 🌫 ☐Hot ☐Cold ☐Mild

Start Time:_____ End Time:_____

Total Duration:_____ Total Distance:_____

Elevation Gain/Loss:_____

Trail Type (circle one):   Out & Back   Loop   One Way / Shuttle

THE HIKE   ☆ ☆ ☆ ☆ ☆

City/State:_____

Trail(s):_____
_____

Start Latitude/Longitude:_____

Terrain:_____

Cell Phone Reception/Carrier:_____

☐First Visit   ☐Return Visit   Personal Rating: Easy / Intermediate / Difficult

Companion(s):_____
_____

Facilities / Water Availability?:_____
_____

Trail & Weather Conditions:_____
_____

Observances (wildlife, nature, views, etc):_____
_____

Gear, Food & Beverages:_____
_____

Notes for next time (shuttles, entrance fees, parking, routes, pets, etc):_____
_____
_____

NOTES / JOURNALING

HIKING LOGBOOK

DATE: ☼ ⛅ ☁ ☂ ⚡ ❄ 🌫 ☐Hot ☐Cold ☐Mild

Start Time:_____ End Time:_____

Total Duration:_____ Total Distance:_____

Elevation Gain/Loss:_____

Trail Type (circle one):   Out & Back   Loop   One Way / Shuttle

THE HIKE ☆☆☆☆☆

City/State:_____

Trail(s):_____

Start Latitude/Longitude:_____

Terrain:_____

Cell Phone Reception/Carrier:_____

☐First Visit   ☐Return Visit   Personal Rating: Easy / Intermediate / Difficult

Companion(s):_____

Facilities / Water Availability?:_____

Trail & Weather Conditions:_____

Observances (wildlife, nature, views, etc):_____

Gear, Food & Beverages:_____

Notes for next time (shuttles, entrance fees, parking, routes, pets, etc):_____

NOTES / JOURNALING

HIKING LOGBOOK

DATE: ☼ ⛅ ☁ ☂ ⛈ ❄ 🌬 ☐Hot ☐Cold ☐Mild

Start Time:_____ End Time:_____

Total Duration:_____ Total Distance:_____

Elevation Gain/Loss:_____

Trail Type (circle one): Out & Back Loop One Way / Shuttle

THE HIKE ☆☆☆☆☆

City/State:_____

Trail(s):_____

Start Latitude/Longitude:_____

Terrain:_____

Cell Phone Reception/Carrier:_____

☐First Visit ☐Return Visit Personal Rating: Easy / Intermediate / Difficult

Companion(s):_____

Facilities / Water Availability?:_____

Trail & Weather Conditions:_____

Observances (wildlife, nature, views, etc):_____

Gear, Food & Beverages:_____

Notes for next time (shuttles, entrance fees, parking, routes, pets, etc):_____

NOTES / JOURNALING

DATE: ☀ ⛅ ☁ 🌧 ⛈ ❄ 🌫 ☐Hot ☐Cold ☐Mild

Start Time:_____ End Time:_____

Total Duration:_____ Total Distance:_____

Elevation Gain/Loss:_____

Trail Type (circle one):   Out & Back   Loop   One Way / Shuttle

THE HIKE   ☆ ☆ ☆ ☆ ☆

City/State:_____

Trail(s):_____

Start Latitude/Longitude:_____

Terrain:_____

Cell Phone Reception/Carrier:_____

☐First Visit   ☐Return Visit   Personal Rating: Easy / Intermediate / Difficult

Companion(s):_____

Facilities / Water Availability?:_____

Trail & Weather Conditions:_____

Observances (wildlife, nature, views, etc):_____

Gear, Food & Beverages:_____

Notes for next time (shuttles, entrance fees, parking, routes, pets, etc):_____
_____

NOTES / JOURNALING

HIKING LOGBOOK

DATE: ☀ ⛅ ☁ ☂ ⛆ ❄ 🌫 ☐Hot ☐Cold ☐Mild

Start Time:_____ End Time:_____

Total Duration:_____ Total Distance:_____

Elevation Gain/Loss:_____

Trail Type (circle one):   Out & Back   Loop   One Way / Shuttle

THE HIKE   ☆ ☆ ☆ ☆ ☆

City/State:_____

Trail(s):_____

_____

Start Latitude/Longitude:_____

Terrain:_____

Cell Phone Reception/Carrier:_____

☐First Visit   ☐Return Visit   Personal Rating: Easy / Intermediate / Difficult

Companion(s):_____

_____

Facilities / Water Availability?:_____

_____

Trail & Weather Conditions:_____

_____

Observances (wildlife, nature, views, etc):_____

_____

Gear, Food & Beverages:_____

_____

Notes for next time (shuttles, entrance fees, parking, routes, pets, etc):_____

_____

_____

NOTES / JOURNALING

HIKING LOGBOOK

DATE: ☐Hot ☐Cold ☐Mild

Start Time:_____ End Time:_____

Total Duration:_____ Total Distance:_____

Elevation Gain/Loss:_____

Trail Type (circle one): Out & Back Loop One Way / Shuttle

THE HIKE ☆☆☆☆☆

City/State:_____

Trail(s):_____
_____

Start Latitude/Longitude:_____

Terrain:_____

Cell Phone Reception/Carrier:_____

☐First Visit ☐Return Visit Personal Rating: Easy / Intermediate / Difficult

Companion(s):_____

Facilities / Water Availability?:_____

Trail & Weather Conditions:_____

Observances (wildlife, nature, views, etc):_____

Gear, Food & Beverages:_____

Notes for next time (shuttles, entrance fees, parking, routes, pets, etc):_____

NOTES / JOURNALING

HIKING LOGBOOK

| DATE: | ☼ ⛅ ☁ 🌢 ⛈ ❄ 🌫 ☐Hot ☐Cold ☐Mild |

Start Time:_____ **End Time:**_____

Total Duration:_____ **Total Distance:**_____

Elevation Gain/Loss:_____

Trail Type (circle one):   Out & Back   Loop   One Way / Shuttle

THE HIKE ☆☆☆☆☆

City/State:_____

Trail(s):_____

Start Latitude/Longitude:_____

Terrain:_____

Cell Phone Reception/Carrier:_____

☐First Visit   ☐Return Visit   **Personal Rating:** Easy / Intermediate / Difficult

Companion(s):_____

Facilities / Water Availability?:_____

Trail & Weather Conditions:_____

Observances (wildlife, nature, views, etc):_____

Gear, Food & Beverages:_____

Notes for next time (shuttles, entrance fees, parking, routes, pets, etc):_____

NOTES / JOURNALING

DATE: ☼ ⛅ ☁ 🌧 ⛈ ❄ 🌫 ☐Hot ☐Cold ☐Mild

Start Time:_____ End Time:_____

Total Duration:_____ Total Distance:_____

Elevation Gain/Loss:_____

Trail Type (circle one):   Out & Back   Loop   One Way / Shuttle

THE HIKE ☆ ☆ ☆ ☆ ☆

City/State:_____

Trail(s):_____
_____

Start Latitude/Longitude:_____

Terrain:_____

Cell Phone Reception/Carrier:_____

☐First Visit   ☐Return Visit   Personal Rating: Easy / Intermediate / Difficult

Companion(s):_____

Facilities / Water Availability?:_____

Trail & Weather Conditions:_____

Observances (wildlife, nature, views, etc):_____

Gear, Food & Beverages:_____

Notes for next time (shuttles, entrance fees, parking, routes, pets, etc):_____
_____

DATE: ☀ ⛅ ☁ 🌦 ⛈ ❄ 🌫 ☐Hot ☐Cold ☐Mild

Start Time:_____ End Time:_____

Total Duration:_____ Total Distance:_____

Elevation Gain/Loss:_____

Trail Type (circle one):   Out & Back   Loop   One Way / Shuttle

THE HIKE ☆☆☆☆☆

City/State:_____

Trail(s):_____

_____

Start Latitude/Longitude:_____

Terrain:_____

Cell Phone Reception/Carrier:_____

☐First Visit ☐Return Visit   Personal Rating: Easy / Intermediate / Difficult

Companion(s):_____

Facilities / Water Availability?:_____

Trail & Weather Conditions:_____

Observances (wildlife, nature, views, etc):_____

Gear, Food & Beverages:_____

Notes for next time (shuttles, entrance fees, parking, routes, pets, etc):_____

_____

DATE: ☀ ⛅ ☁ 🌧 ⛈ ❄ 🌬 ☐Hot ☐Cold ☐Mild

Start Time:_____ End Time:_____

Total Duration:_____ Total Distance:_____

Elevation Gain/Loss:_____

Trail Type (circle one):   Out & Back   Loop   One Way / Shuttle

THE HIKE   ☆ ☆ ☆ ☆ ☆

City/State:_____

Trail(s):_____
_____

Start Latitude/Longitude:_____

Terrain:_____

Cell Phone Reception/Carrier:_____

☐First Visit   ☐Return Visit   Personal Rating: Easy / Intermediate / Difficult

Companion(s):_____

Facilities / Water Availability?:_____

Trail & Weather Conditions:_____

Observances (wildlife, nature, views, etc):_____

Gear, Food & Beverages:_____

Notes for next time (shuttles, entrance fees, parking, routes, pets, etc):_____
_____

NOTES / JOURNALING

HIKING LOGBOOK

DATE: ☼ ⛅ ☁ ☂ ⛈ ❄ 🌬 ☐Hot ☐Cold ☐Mild

Start Time:_____ End Time:_____

Total Duration:_____ Total Distance:_____

Elevation Gain/Loss:_____

Trail Type (circle one):   Out & Back   Loop   One Way / Shuttle

THE HIKE   ☆☆☆☆☆

City/State:_____

Trail(s):_____
_____

Start Latitude/Longitude:_____

Terrain:_____

Cell Phone Reception/Carrier:_____

☐First Visit ☐Return Visit   Personal Rating: Easy / Intermediate / Difficult

Companion(s):_____

Facilities / Water Availability?:_____

Trail & Weather Conditions:_____

Observances (wildlife, nature, views, etc):_____

Gear, Food & Beverages:_____

Notes for next time (shuttles, entrance fees, parking, routes, pets, etc):_____
_____
_____

NOTES / JOURNALING

HIKING LOGBOOK

| DATE: | ☼ ⛅ ☁ 🌧 ⛈ ❄ 🌫 ☐Hot ☐Cold ☐Mild |

Start Time:_____ **End Time:**_____

Total Duration:_____ **Total Distance:**_____

Elevation Gain/Loss:_____

Trail Type (circle one):   Out & Back   Loop   One Way / Shuttle

THE HIKE   ☆ ☆ ☆ ☆ ☆

City/State:_____

Trail(s):_____

_____

Start Latitude/Longitude:_____

Terrain:_____

Cell Phone Reception/Carrier:_____

☐First Visit   ☐Return Visit   Personal Rating: Easy / Intermediate / Difficult

Companion(s):_____

_____

Facilities / Water Availability?:_____

_____

Trail & Weather Conditions:_____

_____

Observances (wildlife, nature, views, etc):_____

_____

Gear, Food & Beverages:_____

_____

Notes for next time (shuttles, entrance fees, parking, routes, pets, etc):_____

_____

_____

NOTES / JOURNALING

HIKING LOGBOOK

DATE: ☼ ⛅ ☁ ☂ ⛈ ❄ 🌬 ☐Hot ☐Cold ☐Mild

Start Time:_____ End Time:_____

Total Duration:_____ Total Distance:_____

Elevation Gain/Loss: _____

Trail Type (circle one):   Out & Back   Loop   One Way / Shuttle

THE HIKE ☆☆☆☆☆

City/State:_____

Trail(s):_____

_____

Start Latitude/Longitude: _____

Terrain: _____

Cell Phone Reception/Carrier: _____

☐First Visit   ☐Return Visit   Personal Rating: Easy / Intermediate / Difficult

Companion(s):_____

_____

Facilities / Water Availability?:_____

_____

Trail & Weather Conditions: _____

_____

Observances (wildlife, nature, views, etc):_____

_____

Gear, Food & Beverages: _____

_____

Notes for next time (shuttles, entrance fees, parking, routes, pets, etc):_____

_____

NOTES / JOURNALING

HIKING LOGBOOK

DATE: ☀ ⛅ ☁ 🌧 ⛈ ❄ 🌬 ☐Hot ☐Cold ☐Mild

Start Time:_____ End Time:_____

Total Duration:_____ Total Distance:_____

Elevation Gain/Loss:_____

Trail Type (circle one):   Out & Back   Loop   One Way / Shuttle

THE HIKE   ☆ ☆ ☆ ☆ ☆

City/State:_____

Trail(s):_____
_____

Start Latitude/Longitude:_____

Terrain:_____

Cell Phone Reception/Carrier:_____

☐First Visit ☐Return Visit   Personal Rating: Easy / Intermediate / Difficult

Companion(s):_____
_____

Facilities / Water Availability?:_____
_____

Trail & Weather Conditions:_____
_____

Observances (wildlife, nature, views, etc):_____
_____

Gear, Food & Beverages:_____
_____

Notes for next time (shuttles, entrance fees, parking, routes, pets, etc):_____
_____
_____

NOTES / JOURNALING

DATE: ☼ ⛅ ☁ 🌧 ⛈ ❄ 🌫 ☐Hot ☐Cold ☐Mild

Start Time:_____ End Time:_____

Total Duration:_____ Total Distance:_____

Elevation Gain/Loss:_____

Trail Type (circle one):   Out & Back   Loop   One Way / Shuttle

THE HIKE ☆☆☆☆☆

City/State:_____

Trail(s):_____
_____

Start Latitude/Longitude:_____

Terrain:_____

Cell Phone Reception/Carrier:_____

☐First Visit ☐Return Visit   Personal Rating: Easy / Intermediate / Difficult

Companion(s):_____
_____

Facilities / Water Availability?:_____
_____

Trail & Weather Conditions:_____
_____

Observances (wildlife, nature, views, etc):_____
_____

Gear, Food & Beverages:_____
_____

Notes for next time (shuttles, entrance fees, parking, routes, pets, etc):_____
_____
_____

NOTES / JOURNALING

HIKING LOGBOOK

DATE: ☼ ⛅ ☁ ☂ ⛈ ❄ 🌫 ☐Hot ☐Cold ☐Mild

Start Time:_____ End Time:_____

Total Duration:_____ Total Distance:_____

Elevation Gain/Loss:_____

Trail Type (circle one):   Out & Back   Loop   One Way / Shuttle

THE HIKE   ☆ ☆ ☆ ☆ ☆

City/State:_____

Trail(s):_____

Start Latitude/Longitude:_____

Terrain:_____

Cell Phone Reception/Carrier:_____

☐First Visit   ☐Return Visit   Personal Rating: Easy / Intermediate / Difficult

Companion(s):_____

Facilities / Water Availability?:_____

Trail & Weather Conditions:_____

Observances (wildlife, nature, views, etc):_____

Gear, Food & Beverages:_____

Notes for next time (shuttles, entrance fees, parking, routes, pets, etc):_____

DATE: ☼ ⛅ ☁ 🌧 ⛈ ❄ 🌫 ☐Hot ☐Cold ☐Mild

Start Time:_____ End Time:_____

Total Duration:_____ Total Distance:_____

Elevation Gain/Loss:_____

Trail Type (circle one):   Out & Back   Loop   One Way / Shuttle

THE HIKE   ☆ ☆ ☆ ☆ ☆

City/State:_____

Trail(s):_____

_____

Start Latitude/Longitude:_____

Terrain:_____

Cell Phone Reception/Carrier:_____

☐First Visit ☐Return Visit   Personal Rating: Easy / Intermediate / Difficult

Companion(s):_____

Facilities / Water Availability?:_____

Trail & Weather Conditions:_____

Observances (wildlife, nature, views, etc):_____

Gear, Food & Beverages:_____

Notes for next time (shuttles, entrance fees, parking, routes, pets, etc):_____
_____

NOTES / JOURNALING

HIKING LOGBOOK

DATE: ☀ ⛅ ☁ 🌧 ⚡ ❄ 🌬 ☐Hot ☐Cold ☐Mild

Start Time:_____ End Time:_____

Total Duration:_____ Total Distance:_____

Elevation Gain/Loss:_____

Trail Type (circle one):   Out & Back   Loop   One Way / Shuttle

THE HIKE   ☆☆☆☆☆

City/State:_____

Trail(s):_____

Start Latitude/Longitude:_____

Terrain:_____

Cell Phone Reception/Carrier:_____

☐First Visit ☐Return Visit   Personal Rating: Easy / Intermediate / Difficult

Companion(s):_____

Facilities / Water Availability?:_____

Trail & Weather Conditions:_____

Observances (wildlife, nature, views, etc):_____

Gear, Food & Beverages:_____

Notes for next time (shuttles, entrance fees, parking, routes, pets, etc):_____

DATE: ☼ ⛅ ☁ ☂ ⛈ ❄ 🌫 ☐Hot ☐Cold ☐Mild

Start Time:_____ End Time:_____

Total Duration:_____ Total Distance:_____

Elevation Gain/Loss:_____

Trail Type (circle one):   Out & Back   Loop   One Way / Shuttle

THE HIKE   ☆ ☆ ☆ ☆ ☆

City/State:_____

Trail(s):_____

_____

Start Latitude/Longitude:_____

Terrain:_____

Cell Phone Reception/Carrier:_____

☐First Visit   ☐Return Visit   Personal Rating: Easy / Intermediate / Difficult

Companion(s):_____

Facilities / Water Availability?:_____

Trail & Weather Conditions:_____

Observances (wildlife, nature, views, etc):_____

Gear, Food & Beverages:_____

Notes for next time (shuttles, entrance fees, parking, routes, pets, etc):_____

_____

HIKING LOGBOOK

DATE: ☼ ⛅ ☁ 🌧 ⛈ ❄ 🌫 ☐Hot ☐Cold ☐Mild

Start Time: _____ **End Time:** _____

Total Duration: _____ **Total Distance:** _____

Elevation Gain/Loss: _____

Trail Type (circle one):   Out & Back   Loop   One Way / Shuttle

THE HIKE ☆☆☆☆☆

City/State: _____

Trail(s): _____
_____
_____

Start Latitude/Longitude: _____

Terrain: _____

Cell Phone Reception/Carrier: _____

☐First Visit   ☐Return Visit   Personal Rating: Easy / Intermediate / Difficult

Companion(s): _____

Facilities / Water Availability?: _____

Trail & Weather Conditions: _____

Observances (wildlife, nature, views, etc): _____

Gear, Food & Beverages: _____

Notes for next time (shuttles, entrance fees, parking, routes, pets, etc): _____
_____

HIKING LOGBOOK

DATE: ☼ ⛅ ☁ ☂ ⛈ ❄ 🌫 ☐Hot ☐Cold ☐Mild

Start Time:_____ End Time:_____

Total Duration:_____ Total Distance:_____

Elevation Gain/Loss:_____

Trail Type (circle one): Out & Back Loop One Way / Shuttle

THE HIKE ☆☆☆☆☆

City/State:_____

Trail(s):_____
_____

Start Latitude/Longitude:_____

Terrain:_____

Cell Phone Reception/Carrier:_____

☐First Visit ☐Return Visit Personal Rating: Easy / Intermediate / Difficult

Companion(s):_____

Facilities / Water Availability?:_____

Trail & Weather Conditions:_____

Observances (wildlife, nature, views, etc):_____

Gear, Food & Beverages:_____

Notes for next time (shuttles, entrance fees, parking, routes, pets, etc):_____

NOTES / JOURNALING

DATE: ☀ ⛅ ☁ 🌧 ⛈ ❄ 🌬 ☐Hot ☐Cold ☐Mild

Start Time:_____ End Time:_____

Total Duration:_____Total Distance:_____

Elevation Gain/Loss: _____

Trail Type (circle one):   Out & Back   Loop   One Way / Shuttle

THE HIKE ☆☆☆☆☆

City/State:_____

Trail(s):_____
_____

Start Latitude/Longitude: _____

Terrain:_____

Cell Phone Reception/Carrier:_____

☐First Visit   ☐Return Visit   Personal Rating: Easy / Intermediate / Difficult

Companion(s):_____
_____

Facilities / Water Availability?:_____
_____

Trail & Weather Conditions: _____
_____

Observances (wildlife, nature, views, etc):_____
_____

Gear, Food & Beverages:_____
_____

Notes for next time (shuttles, entrance fees, parking, routes, pets, etc):_____
_____
_____

NOTES / JOURNALING

HIKING LOGBOOK

DATE: ☀ ⛅ ☁ 🌦 ⛈ ❄ 🌬 ☐Hot ☐Cold ☐Mild

Start Time:_____ End Time:_____

Total Duration:_____ Total Distance:_____

Elevation Gain/Loss:_____

Trail Type (circle one): Out & Back   Loop   One Way / Shuttle

THE HIKE ☆☆☆☆☆

City/State:_____

Trail(s):_____

Start Latitude/Longitude:_____

Terrain:_____

Cell Phone Reception/Carrier:_____

☐First Visit ☐Return Visit   Personal Rating: Easy / Intermediate / Difficult

Companion(s):_____

Facilities / Water Availability?:_____

Trail & Weather Conditions:_____

Observances (wildlife, nature, views, etc):_____

Gear, Food & Beverages:_____

Notes for next time (shuttles, entrance fees, parking, routes, pets, etc):_____

NOTES / JOURNALING

HIKING LOGBOOK

DATE: ☀ ⛅ ☁ 🌧 🌦 ❄ 🌫 ☐Hot ☐Cold ☐Mild

Start Time:_____ End Time:_____

Total Duration:_____ Total Distance:_____

Elevation Gain/Loss:_____

Trail Type (circle one):   Out & Back   Loop   One Way / Shuttle

THE HIKE ☆☆☆☆☆

City/State:_____

Trail(s):_____

Start Latitude/Longitude:_____

Terrain:_____

Cell Phone Reception/Carrier:_____

☐First Visit   ☐Return Visit   Personal Rating: Easy / Intermediate / Difficult

Companion(s):_____

Facilities / Water Availability?:_____

Trail & Weather Conditions:_____

Observances (wildlife, nature, views, etc):_____

Gear, Food & Beverages:_____

Notes for next time (shuttles, entrance fees, parking, routes, pets, etc):_____

NOTES / JOURNALING

DATE: ☀ ⛅ ☁ 🌧 ⛈ ❄ 🌫 ☐Hot ☐Cold ☐Mild

Start Time:_____ End Time:_____

Total Duration:_____ Total Distance:_____

Elevation Gain/Loss:_____

Trail Type (circle one):   Out & Back   Loop   One Way / Shuttle

THE HIKE ☆☆☆☆☆

City/State:_____

Trail(s):_____
_____

Start Latitude/Longitude:_____

Terrain:_____

Cell Phone Reception/Carrier:_____

☐First Visit ☐Return Visit   Personal Rating: Easy / Intermediate / Difficult

Companion(s):_____

Facilities / Water Availability?:_____

Trail & Weather Conditions:_____

Observances (wildlife, nature, views, etc):_____

Gear, Food & Beverages:_____

Notes for next time (shuttles, entrance fees, parking, routes, pets, etc):_____
_____

HIKING LOGBOOK

DATE: ☼ ⛅ ☁ 🌧 ⛈ ❄ 🌬 ☐Hot ☐Cold ☐Mild

Start Time:_____ End Time:_____

Total Duration:_____ Total Distance:_____

Elevation Gain/Loss:_____

Trail Type (circle one):   Out & Back   Loop   One Way / Shuttle

THE HIKE   ☆ ☆ ☆ ☆ ☆

City/State:_____

Trail(s):_____
_____

Start Latitude/Longitude:_____

Terrain:_____

Cell Phone Reception/Carrier:_____

☐First Visit   ☐Return Visit   Personal Rating: Easy / Intermediate / Difficult

Companion(s):_____
_____

Facilities / Water Availability?:_____
_____

Trail & Weather Conditions:_____
_____

Observances (wildlife, nature, views, etc):_____
_____

Gear, Food & Beverages:_____
_____

Notes for next time (shuttles, entrance fees, parking, routes, pets, etc):_____
_____
_____

NOTES / JOURNALING

HIKING LOGBOOK

DATE: ☼ ⛅ ☁ ☂ ⛈ ❄ 🌫 ☐Hot ☐Cold ☐Mild

Start Time:_____ End Time:_____

Total Duration:_____ Total Distance:_____

Elevation Gain/Loss:_____

Trail Type (circle one):   Out & Back   Loop   One Way / Shuttle

THE HIKE ☆☆☆☆☆

City/State:_____

Trail(s):_____
_____

Start Latitude/Longitude: _____

Terrain: _____

Cell Phone Reception/Carrier: _____

☐First Visit   ☐Return Visit   Personal Rating: Easy / Intermediate / Difficult

Companion(s): _____
_____

Facilities / Water Availability?: _____
_____

Trail & Weather Conditions: _____
_____

Observances (wildlife, nature, views, etc): _____
_____

Gear, Food & Beverages: _____
_____

Notes for next time (shuttles, entrance fees, parking, routes, pets, etc): _____
_____
_____

NOTES / JOURNALING

HIKING LOGBOOK

DATE: ☼ ⛅ ☁ 🌦 🌧 ❄ 🌫 ☐Hot ☐Cold ☐Mild

Start Time:_____ End Time:_____

Total Duration:_____ Total Distance:_____

Elevation Gain/Loss:_____

Trail Type (circle one):   Out & Back   Loop   One Way / Shuttle

THE HIKE   ☆☆☆☆☆

City/State:_____

Trail(s):_____

_____

Start Latitude/Longitude:_____

Terrain:_____

Cell Phone Reception/Carrier:_____

☐First Visit   ☐Return Visit   Personal Rating: Easy / Intermediate / Difficult

Companion(s):_____

_____

Facilities / Water Availability?:_____

_____

Trail & Weather Conditions:_____

_____

Observances (wildlife, nature, views, etc):_____

_____

Gear, Food & Beverages:_____

_____

Notes for next time (shuttles, entrance fees, parking, routes, pets, etc):____

_____

_____

NOTES / JOURNALING

HIKING LOGBOOK

DATE: ☼ ⛅ ☁ 🌧 ⛈ ❄ 🌬 ☐Hot ☐Cold ☐Mild

Start Time:_____ End Time:_____

Total Duration:_____ Total Distance:_____

Elevation Gain/Loss:_____

Trail Type (circle one):   Out & Back   Loop   One Way / Shuttle

THE HIKE   ☆ ☆ ☆ ☆ ☆

City/State:_____

Trail(s):_____
_____

Start Latitude/Longitude:_____

Terrain:_____

Cell Phone Reception/Carrier:_____

☐First Visit   ☐Return Visit   Personal Rating: Easy / Intermediate / Difficult

Companion(s):_____

Facilities / Water Availability?:_____

Trail & Weather Conditions:_____

Observances (wildlife, nature, views, etc):_____

Gear, Food & Beverages:_____

Notes for next time (shuttles, entrance fees, parking, routes, pets, etc):_____
_____

NOTES / JOURNALING

HIKING LOGBOOK

| **DATE:** | ☀ ⛅ ☁ 🌧 ⛈ ❄ 🌬 ☐Hot ☐Cold ☐Mild |

Start Time:_____ **End Time:**_____

Total Duration:_____ **Total Distance:**_____

Elevation Gain/Loss:_____

Trail Type (circle one):   Out & Back   Loop   One Way / Shuttle

THE HIKE ☆ ☆ ☆ ☆ ☆

City/State:_____

Trail(s):_____
_____

Start Latitude/Longitude:_____

Terrain:_____

Cell Phone Reception/Carrier:_____

☐First Visit ☐Return Visit   Personal Rating: Easy / Intermediate / Difficult

Companion(s):_____
_____

Facilities / Water Availability?:_____
_____

Trail & Weather Conditions:_____
_____

Observances (wildlife, nature, views, etc):_____
_____

Gear, Food & Beverages:_____
_____

Notes for next time (shuttles, entrance fees, parking, routes, pets, etc):_____
_____

NOTES / JOURNALING

DATE: ☀ ⛅ ☁ 🌧 ⛈ ❄ 🌫 ☐Hot ☐Cold ☐Mild

Start Time:_____ End Time:_____

Total Duration:_____ Total Distance:_____

Elevation Gain/Loss:_____

Trail Type (circle one):   Out & Back   Loop   One Way / Shuttle

THE HIKE   ☆ ☆ ☆ ☆ ☆

City/State:_____

Trail(s):_____
_____

Start Latitude/Longitude:_____

Terrain:_____

Cell Phone Reception/Carrier:_____

☐First Visit   ☐Return Visit   Personal Rating: Easy / Intermediate / Difficult

Companion(s):_____
_____

Facilities / Water Availability?:_____
_____

Trail & Weather Conditions: _____
_____

Observances (wildlife, nature, views, etc):_____
_____

Gear, Food & Beverages: _____
_____

Notes for next time (shuttles, entrance fees, parking, routes, pets, etc):_____
_____
_____

NOTES / JOURNALING

HIKING LOGBOOK

DATE: ☼ ⛅ ☁ ☔ 🌧 ❄ 🌬 ☐Hot ☐Cold ☐Mild

Start Time:_____ End Time:_____

Total Duration:_____ Total Distance:_____

Elevation Gain/Loss:_____

Trail Type (circle one): Out & Back   Loop   One Way / Shuttle

THE HIKE ☆ ☆ ☆ ☆ ☆

City/State:_____

Trail(s):_____

_____

Start Latitude/Longitude: _____

Terrain: _____

Cell Phone Reception/Carrier:_____

☐First Visit ☐Return Visit   Personal Rating: Easy / Intermediate / Difficult

Companion(s):_____

_____

Facilities / Water Availability?:_____

_____

Trail & Weather Conditions:_____

_____

Observances (wildlife, nature, views, etc):_____

_____

Gear, Food & Beverages:_____

_____

Notes for next time (shuttles, entrance fees, parking, routes, pets, etc):_____

_____

_____

NOTES / JOURNALING